CIVIL WAR RECOLLI

JEFF DAVIS PIE

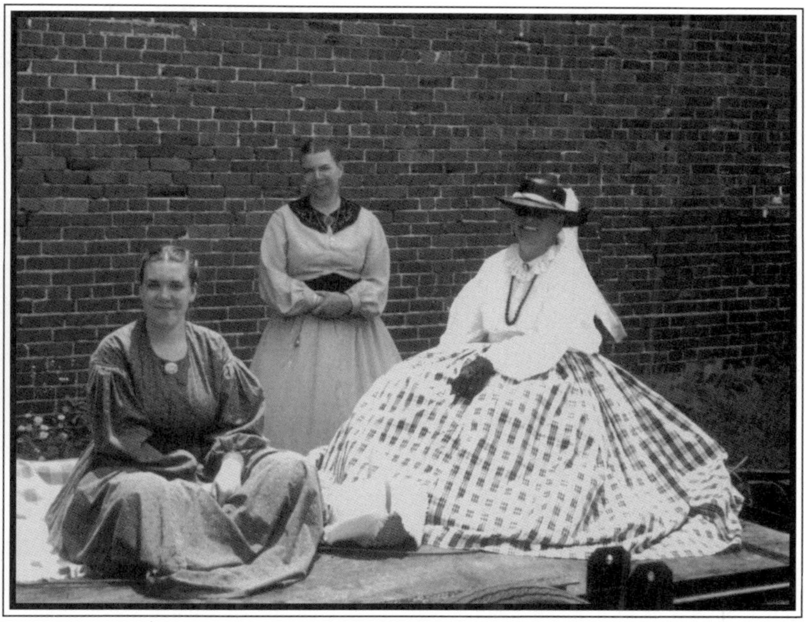

A Saga of Significant, First-time Events
in "The War Between The States"

By Robert E. Anderson, PhD

ACKNOWLEDGEMENTS

All photos and sketches are the work of the author except for the West Virginia Archives photo, Figure 1, page 48.

Front cover: Belington re-enactors.

Rear cover : Philippi covered bridge, built by Lemuel Cheneweth in 1852, and then restored in the 1990's after a fire in 1989.

A special thanks to Mrs. Darlene Ford, of the Taylor County Historical Society, for her interest and encouragement.

~~~~~~~~~~~~~~~~~

To Kristin and Jamie, my grandchildren, and in special memory of all the many children who suffered in the Civil War.

Second Printing 2004

Registered in the Library of Congress. ISBN: 0-9717976-1-7
~~~~~~~~~~~~~~~~~

CONTENTS

PREFACE

Our bloody Civil War was devastating. Losses of human life and personal property on both sides were widespread. The war was a fire storm over America for more than four years, ending in 1865.

Over this period, as with any epic, there were those significant firsts, certain beginnings of human suffering and yes, some human achievements that would benefit the survivors after the last cannon shot was heard.

This book is about some of those Civil War firsts.

INTRODUCTION

The setting for our trip back in time is western Virginia. The year is 1861. Kansas has just joined the Union as our 34th state. Its state constitution supports the North. Meanwhile, in Mississippi, US Senator Jefferson Davis is about to resign from Congress to become the President of the rebellious Confederacy.

Imagine for a moment. You live in western Virginia in April, 1861; and you read: "All connection between Virginia and the Federal government is dissolved." !!!

How would you react? If you were alive then, how do you think your neighbors would react?

To witness some of those events and tensions of that time, our modern-day Ben Williams goes back in time with you; to witness some of the action where the war began.

And now our story.

~~~~~~~~~~~~~~~~~~~~~~~~~~~~
~~~~~~~~~~~~~~~~~~~~~~~~~~~~

CHAPTER 1

A Visit to Pruntytown

It was a typical early morning in late August. The West Virginia sun had just burnt off the last traces of valley fog that hovered over Maple Lake.

"Goo--od," said Ben Williams to himself out loud. He surveyed the outdoor scene. His watch showed 7:15. "Time to get moving if I'm going to the flea market early."

Ben was referring to the annual Pruntytown flea market held each year in that Taylor County hamlet, 12 miles down the road from his house at the lake.

For many years during the last weekend in August, the flea market attracted thousands of shoppers and scores of vendors from all over, including the surrounding states. Ben knew of some buyers who would come each year from as far away as California and New York.

Ben was a retired teacher and spent most of his time gardening, jogging and reading Civil War history. Occasionally, he wrote but never published anything ... only personal notes as a hobby ... kept privately to himself.

Pruntytown held special intrigue for Ben; partly, it was because this sleepy village of 500 or so was a prior hot bed of activity during our "War of the Rebellion". Also he was concerned events of that time had long-since gone unnoticed in the annals of history.

Pruntytown at one time was the county seat. It boasted of having a successful college in the 1840's and 50's ... Rector College, long before Fairmont State or West Virginia University got their starts as normal schools.

Nowadays, in the year 2000, Pruntytown is the tranquil setting of country churches, cross-roads businesses and a state-run juvenile detention-rehabilitation center.

Ben kissed his wife, Jan, goodbye and jumped into his car. The flea market site was only 5 minutes away, and he arrived as he had planned, about 8 AM. The flea market was located just across the road from the re-hab center.

The seventy or more vendors were already set upon the open field, about 10 rows of them. Parking was beginning to become a problem, but Ben found a place, nearby.

He stepped from his car, tapped his remote locking device and received an audible reply from his car horn.

Ben eagerly made his way to the first row of tables.

He walked past the first 3, nodding hello to each vendor as he passed them. But, he didn't stop. They each had tools for sale. Good tools, Ben thought. Good buys for others but not for him this day. Ben was looking for an old book or two, something preferably on local history.

Passing some fresh produce tables, he stopped at the last one in the first row. The crowds were still sparse, not elbow to elbow.

Ben hated wall to wall shopping congestion. The thought of it routinely kept him out of many malls and shopping centers.

At the last table, he noticed a pile or two of used books. "Well, this is a good place to start," He greeted the vendor. "Good morning!"

Sarah, the vendor, replied. "Hi, welcome. My name's Sarah!"

Ben introduced himself. She was a cheery fifty-some, he thought with a healthy, ruddy complexion. It glowed a bit when Ben asked if she had any history books.

"Well, I have these here," she gestured.

But, Ben could see they were primarily old school text books, and he wasn't too interested in them. He pointed with his finger. "What's in that box?"

"Oh, that's somethin' I just heven't gottin' around tuh sort out yet," Sarah said as she reached for the box. She opened it in front of Ben and flushed some more. She could sense his developing interest in the contents.

Inside the old cigar box were some loose greeting cards postmarked in the fifties. Not too interested in these, he leafed carefully beneath two old pictures. There was an old yellow piece of letterhead paper.

Ben could make out the words, "Pruntytown and County of Taylor" at the top. He turned it around. There was a signature, but he could only make out the first name. It was "Fabricius" somebody and __ atham, Commanding. But he did make out the date. It was 1861! Ben pretended to be less interested.

He slowly looked further through the dusty pile in the box. He passed some old recipes for cakes and meat dishes. Some he had never heard of before. He came to a tattered old office folio, a thick cardboard type envelope tied with string. More recipes, he thought.

Sarah glanced sideways and pursed her lips. "Got 'em at an auction last week here in the Flemington area, she mentioned. "Ah, ohhhh, I'd take twenty-five dollars for them."

Ben shot a friendly glance back at her, smiled, but said nothing. He undid the cardboard envelope flap and pulled out a yellowed sheet of folded composition paper. It had hand-written dates and entries ... looks like diary pages, Ben thought to himself.

Ben didn't act too interested at this point. "Sarah, I could only afford ten," he countered with a smile.

Sarah wrinkled her forehead as if indifferent and it appeared she was going to refuse. She surprised Ben with, "O.K.That'll be ten dollars and sixty cents with tax, please."

He handed her the exact amount, and she handed him the box in a plastic bag with a cheerful "thank you" and smile. He said, "So long! Nice to meet you! ... hope to see you again next year."

Sarah called after him, "Oh It is a small world; maybe ; maybe even sooner, Ben Williams !"

Ben smiled again and waved at her. He saw nothing else he wanted ... He wasn't even sure why he wanted this old box of someone else's discards. But the name, "Fabricius" and the date intrigued him.

He hurried away and went briskly, but politely through the rest of the vendors' set-ups and tables. He bought nothing else.The sun had now climbed high in the sky. It was about 10 AM.

And with the warmth of the midmorning sun, came the thickening crowds of people that milled about. “It is time to leave,” Ben said aloud. “Time to leave.” And, he smilingly waved good-bye to the last vendor.

He then left the site and returned to his car. Once inside, Ben did not immediately start the engine. As he sat behind the wheel, he looked at his recent purchase from Sarah.

Five recipes in the cigar box came to his attention. One of them was for “Pigeon Pie;” another, “Belgian Hare Salad.” A note penciled along-side it read: “Housewives may not recognize these in the market, because the hares are first skinned for their furs and sold naked. These rabbits are also canned and sold as labeled ‘Boned Turkey’. ”

His eyes then caught the third recipe. It was for “Bewitched Liver.”

Another called for a 20 cent beef shank and a 2 cent loaf of bread as ingredients in a version of “Brunswick Stew.”

“Really exact measurements,” he said and loudly laughed. He didn’t look at the fifth which was most significant.

Amused, Ben thought Jan would get a kick out of them also.He laughed loudly and added, “Well, whatever will she do with these! ... maybe spring one on some of her bridge cronies ... as a joke, at her next covered dish affair.

There are a couple in the country club ... ones who would really appreciate naked Belgian Hare!

Ben laughed again. The thought of food made him both hungry and sleepy. Before he realized it, he was out of the car again. He had this urge to get something to munch on. Over there ... the food stand in the old jail museum, he thought.

And, he headed across the street toward the old, historic jailhouse where a startling surprise awaited him.

~~~~~~~~~~~~~~~~~~~~~~~
~~~~~~~~~~~~~~~~~~~~~~~

CHAPTER 2

A Special Slice of Pie

The old brick jailhouse had been renovated by the local historical society The historic, old building was now a prominent tour point along the Civil War trail in West Virginia.

Now a museum and gift shop, it had once served as a prison for unruly whites and black slaves before the war. During the 1860's, it had been a safe house refuge for runaway slaves to hide them temporarily before their escapes after dark to the North.

Once inside, Ben was refreshed by the the more comfortable, cool temperature in the building. A shop-keeper volunteer approached him and greeted him with a smile and "Hello."

"Would you like to try a free sample of our specialty? We're selling 9 ounce pies of this dessert today."

The clerk, in her thirties, was dressed in period clothes: a full-length flowing blue gingham skirt with a high lace collar. She was also wearing a gray apron and a matching bonnet with white lace.

Ben nodded and replied, "Yes, I'll be glad to try it."

She smiled again and placed a generous wedge of pie on a plate and put it in front of Ben at the counter along with a fork and napkin.

"It is called 'Jeff Davis Pie'," she added. "There ... Some pink lemonade also to go along with it, Sir ?"

Ben replied, "Yes, and thank you!"

He took a forkful of the pie. Its texture, somewhat like a baked custard. It was tasty, with a nut-like sweet flavor; it was good. He was about to wash it down with a lengthy drink of the lemonade when he became very dizzy. The room and the waitress began to spin around and around ...

Ben grabbed the countertop edge for support, but some force pulled him away and threw him through the air across the shop to the floor. He was half-conscious. The lights in the ceiling had a glaring rainbow glow and seemed to be coming towards him ...

Then, suddenly there was a tug at his arm. "This way, this way," called a hoarse feminine voice to him. "Come! You must follow me before it wears off !"

There was a familiarity to her voice, but Ben's vision was fuzzy. He could not make out any features in the building. The woman helped him to his feet where he landed and quickly led him to a trapdoor in the floor.

With one hand, she opened the trapdoor and tugged at him again with the other. She disappeared into the square black hole, down a flight of old wooden steps into the darkness below. Ben felt compelled by some force to stumble after her.

He was confused; dumbfounded. But, his sight and balance were gradually returning. He was in an old musty-smelling tunnel under the old jailhouse. As he walked forward following the woman, he broke through old dangling cob-webs.

Ben stumbled to catch up and barely made out her shadowy outline in the blackness ahead. They had gone about twenty feet underground, when suddenly they came to a right angle bend. There, ahead about fifty paces or so, was a distant light ... daylight!

As he approached, the bright hole got bigger and bigger to him. He could see a grassy clearing, and human figures walking; and some were on horseback.

There was quite a crowd milling about. Some calling; some shouting.

It appeared to be some kind of staging area, as if some group was getting ready to line up for a patriotic parade or similar event. Ben could now see flags and hear military music.

"Where am I?" he wondered to himself out loud.

~~~~~~~~~~~~~~~~~~~~~~~~~~~~~~
~~~~~~~~~~~~~~~~~~~~~~~~~~~~~~

CHAPTER 3

Muster Days

Ben made his way out of the tunnel. The light was blinding bright. After his eyes adjusted, Ben noticed men in uniform and others mingling in front of a courthouse. Up front an elderly, gray-bearded fellow bedecked with war medals on his chest was shaking his fist and making a point.

"For the Union," he was saying. "For the Union! We must now protect and drive away the cowardly Rebels who would threaten our wives, our children, our homes and our land!"

Civil War re-enactors rehearsing for the flea market's afternoon program, Ben thought.

A large cheer went up from the crowd in response to the old bearded warrior.

Ben turned to a young man at his elbow. “Who is that fellow?” he asked.

“Why, don’t you know?” came the reply. “That’s my father, John Cather who fought in the Mexican War in 1847,” the proud son added. “M’name’s F. A. Cather. Many just call me ‘Fabe’. What’s yours?”

If it was one thing Ben didn’t like it was a “wise guy” who made “Smart Alec” remarks when one asked an innocent question. “1847, huh! Well, the old boy has certainly aged well over the last hundred and fifty years,” Ben quipped. “Ben’s my name; Ben William;” he held out his hand to shake “Fabe’s.”

A female voice behind Ben spoke out above the din. “Ben, welcome to the year, 1861.”

It was a familiar voice, the one belonging to the woman who led him here ... through the tunnel ... to this clearing! And then he received a further surprise when Ben turned around. It was Sarah; Sarah, the flea market vendor! Only, her manner of speech was more polished.

“Where did you come from?” he stammered.

“Hello again, Ben Williams,” she replied, ignoring his question.

“Mother, you know this stranger?” “Fabe” asked.

“Yes. His name is Ben Williams. He’s all right. You can trust him, son. He’s from the other side.”

Ben didn't exactly understand what she meant. But, with that, each man extended and shook hands. "Well Ben, I'm proud to meet you. Today is Federal Day here in Pruntytown."

Ben nodded as if to agree with "Fabe" and go along with the practical joke. (He means Flea Market Day.) Ben thought.

But before he could say anything, Sarah grabbed his arm. "Come with me," she said as she looked at her son. "Not again," was Ben's response.

"Please excuse us, 'Fabe'," she continued. "We need to go over to the church and discuss some plans. Send your father over as soon as he is finished."
(Her son nodded.)

"Fabe" and Ben looked a little puzzled, but couldn't argue. Sarah was too forceful. Ben shrugged his shoulders. All this joking around about 1847 and 1861...

Sarah still tugged a bit at Ben as he hesitantly crossed the road with her. Being led away by a woman without apparent reason was not his cup of tea. What's this all about, he thought. What's coming next, here?

He did not have to wait long enough for answers. As soon as they were inside in the privacy of the sanctuary, Sarah motioned to the rear pews.

"Here, this back pew will do. You sit here, Ben and I'll be across the aisle." She sat down across the aisle from him; and what followed, what she unfolded, was unbelievable.

"Ben, you will have trouble believing this, but you are back in time. Today is May 15, 1861.

"And we are at a Union muster in Pruntytown," she continued, " just before the start of the Civil War ..."

Ben stared at her. Then he abruptly got up to leave. "You need help, Sarah," he said softly and pitifully.

"No! Wait. Hear me out," Sarah pleaded. "Don't go out there, yet. You'll be killed, because you stand out as a stranger. And these days, strangers in the eyes of us locals, have no trunk or business around here except to stir up trouble. They stand out like rascals, like bush-whackers, like spies.

"Wait, listen to me!" she implored.

Ben was astonished. "Sarah, how could this be? You expect me to believe that I've traveled through some time warp back over a hundred years ago, back to the 1860's?"

"Yes," she replied. "It happened when you ate the 'Jeff Davis Pie'! You reacted; or it reacted. You, you are a sensitive; one who can relate to those of us on the other side."

"And I want to make sure no harm comes to you while you are here in this century."

Ben shivered; a cold, quivering feeling went from the back of his shoulders down his spine. "But Sarah ... you, your booth, the flea market ...You were there. I bought the old stuff !"

Sarah looked into his eyes and cocked her head to one side. "Ben, I'm from both worlds. But I am only seen by a few of your generation from whence you came," she laughed as she repeated her words. "I even sound different in your world than I do here."

~~~~~~~~~~~~~~~~~~~~~~
~~~~~~~~~~~~~~~~~~~~~~

CHAPTER 4

"Are You With Us?"

Ben was totally confused. "But how? When?" So confused he didn't even know how to ask the right questions.

"Ben," Sarah cautioned. "You must be very careful to avoid making opinionated statements while here. Listening is always best in a strange place.

"Observe and learn and accept where you are.

"Now, come along. People will start to wonder about us if they find us alone here ... even in a church, busy-bodies misunderstand and spread gossip.That didn't change with the ages," she sighed with a short laugh.

As they both stepped outside the church the clamor and clatter seemed to be louder than before.

Suddenly "Fabe," now on horseback, rode up to them.

"Look. Look," he said. "There's that no-good Adolphus.

'Fabe' continued. "There he is, across the lawn with that Hasbrough making seditious speeches against our people and our country. Trying to sign up Confederate troops, they are. You remember, Ben, You saw his name at Mother's booth."

"You ... you know about the booth?" Ben responded.

"Yes, I know, Ben. But Mother and I are the only ones who know, and it will be better to let it be that way. Right, Mother?"

Sarah nodded affirmatively.

Ben looked back at the flea market site. But there was no evidence of any! No flea market in progress!

His eyes swept from left to right, beyond the hole in the sodden hillside, the tunnel exit where he had just emerged. No flea market vendors, no crowd of lookers, no buyers such as the crowd of people he had just left.

Instead of the concrete paved road of US Route 250, there was only a dirt, one-lane track ... and no automobiles ... not even his!

Sarah seemed to sense Ben's confusion and loss of place.

She touched his right sleeve and said, “Ben, everything will come out in the clear in due time. Don’t expect all the answers now.

We don’t know why the Almighty has given you this gift and has sent you back here ... maybe as a witness.”

Ben seemed somewhat comforted by her words.

“Ben, here’s someone I want you to meet. He’s coming over here with my husband, John, who I also want you to meet. Remember, no one else knows you are from the 21st century, except ‘Fabe’.”

Sarah continued, “Hello, John! I see you brought George Latham with you. Fine speech, Dear! Judging from the cheers and applause and the end, the crowd liked it.”

“Thank you, Dear,” John Cather replied.

“Yes, John did a good job,” offered George Latham ...” We got at least 24 more sign ups in the Grafton Guards.”

George was a resident of Grafton. He was respected among Union supporters. He served as Delegate of the people and recently returned from Union-supported musters in Clarksburg.

Sarah smiled at both. “I want you to meet a newly found friend, Ben Williams,” she said.

The men then shook hands all around.

"Are you with us, Mr. Williams?" John Cather squinted at Ben. His steel blue eyes penetrated Ben's glance for some sign or signal of Ben's inner-most thoughts.

Again, Ben shivered slightly. A cagey person, this Cather, he thought.

Sarah came to his rescue. "Why, Dear! I said he is a friend."

Ben gathered himself. "Mr. Cather, I assure you, sir, I didn't come here to fight against you and your son."

Latham smiled and said, "Gooood! We can use all the home support we can get. I invite you to be with us at every meeting and muster."

Sarah responded, "Well, that's good to hear. Ben has traveled a long way in the last day. You must be tired, Ben."

Ben did feel weary and said as much to the group.

"Well then, for now, you must rest. Come with me to Widow Poling's place," offered "Fabe." "She has a clean quiet place where you can rest.

"You will need it, because later this afternoon, is going to be a big day! As we said, Federal Muster Day here in Pruntytown!"

Ben felt weak and dizzy again. He had heard all that was said and still couldn't believe any of it.

He was so tired, so sleepy. Suddenly, the next thing he knew, he was at Widow Poling's, rolling over in a strange, but comfortable, clean bed with a tick mattress and soon, fast asleep taking a mid day nap.

The widow had a small cottage not far from the jail and near the center of all the noise and clamor made by voices for both sides as they attempted to to sign up volunteers for their sides to fight in the impending war.

It seemed as though he had just dozed off. "Ben! Ben!" he heard, as his name was called louder and louder. It was Sarah Cather! It can't be, he thought. I just laid down. But, there she was; impatiently shaking him. "Let's go," she said ... as he stumbled to the door in her shadow.

Out on the street in front of Widow Poling's, crowds were gathering. A man in his sixties or seventies was holding several copies of the Grafton newspaper high above his head. "Here's the latest from Richmond ... Letcher wants war," he yelled, referring to the Confederate sympathizer, Governor Letcher of Virginia.

Sarah remarked, "That Letcher is a fool. Why, do you know he even asked his Confederate Colonel Porterfield to seize the B&O railroad?"

"All the way from here to Harpers Ferry," she continued. "Imagine the nerve of that Letcher! That should sit well with the B & O railroad bosses, since they are for Lincoln and the Union.

"See, over there ..." she pointed for Ben, "That's Lawyer Humphreys," she pointed. "Always was a Rebel even as a boy. He's tryin' to sign up men to fight against us.

"Only last month, Delegate Burdett warned us of the back-stabbin' Governor Letcher and his Richmond government. Here, lets see what Mr. Latham has to say after hearing Burdette's report. Sarah read it to the others:

" 'The Call to Create a New State in Western Virginia'."

She continued ... **" 'It is timely we think of separation from the Mother state and to forming a new state '."**

Ben responded to Sarah. "Latham seems to be writing what everyone around here keeps saying, except for that Humphreys person over there."

"Well," Sarah responded. "There are many people on both sides, not many Rebels, 'Seceshes' (secessionists) we call them, for the South around these parts.

"Here in Pruntytown, a Confederate rally has caused a lot of commotion. Some Rebels have mustered into Letcher's Guards, loyal to the Governor."

"And, from the Clarksburg area, we even hear of a Rebel Harrison Guards unit headin' our way to take Grafton.

"So, we live in a dangerous time, when neighbor is threatening neighbor."

Sarah could have also told Ben that, on this day: May 15th, Confederate Col. Porterfield reported to General Robert E. Lee he had no regular troops in Grafton and only a handful of volunteers from the Pruntytown / Fetterman area.

Porterfield was later to write: "I found myself alone in a county, hostile to the South ... without money or supplies of any kind."

So badly equipped were these would-be troops, they were nicknamed the "Tin Cup Soldiers" by Sarah and her friends.

Nonetheless, Rebel reinforcements were on the way, and would arrive within the week to try to stir up trouble on May 22nd and 23rd.

"Dangerous times," Ben repeated. "Yes, I can see trouble is certainly brewing."

As if on cue, the air near Ben was punctured by pistol shots and yelling by an approaching fellow in Union uniform. "Hey, 'Fabe' listen to this," he was saying. "Listen to this," he yelled again. He was in his early thirties and holding a shiny pistol above his head.

"Fabe" Cather smiled and in return, greeted his friend. "Happy Birthday ! Oh, celebrating early, 'Thorny'?"

It was Private Thornsbury Bailey Brown, one of the local recruiters and member of the pro-Union Grafton Guards. Today was also his 32nd birthday.

"I just signed up the Willhide and Simpson boys, six all told," Bailey Brown announced with a wild look of triumph in his eyes.

"Let um all come from Richmond, I say." Brown fired another round. "We be ready and will give Lee and Jeff Davis a warm reception.

"Who yuh got here, 'Fabe' ?... Ah mean Lt. Cather ... this'un in the funny-lookin' clothes." Bailey glared at Ben in a menacing way.

"Whoa, 'Thorny'". "Fabe" was trying to rein in the charged-up soldier, somewhat. "Stop wavin' your new pistol around like that. You'll hurt some innocent person, 'Thorny.' Ben's a friend. T. Bailey Brown, meet Ben Williams."

Ben slowly extended his hand and said: "Hello, 'Thorny'."

Brown held his hand out, cautiously. He had a tight-lipped smile pasted on his face. "Pleased to make your acquaintance, I'm sure," he said ... very formally and stiffly.

And then brashly added, "But call me: Bailey or Mr. Brown, he demanded; "not 'Thorny.' I save 'Thorny' only for best friends and family ... maybe after we git to know each other better ..."

Ben thought this was strange ... this formal, pointed greeting. Ben thought: a rather cold individual; one probably given to snap judgements and mood swings ... It seemed he was out to prove his manhood to the world.

To cover his thoughts, Ben smiled and added, "Happy birthday, Mr. Brown. Is that a new birthday present?"

Bailey Brown relaxed somewhat. "Yep, and a new holster, too from my uncle and aunt. Well, I see some young bucks over cheer (there) so I'd best be off to sign um up. Here have a sip of good 'mountain dew' afore I go." Brown reached for and offered his hip flask to "Fabe" and Ben.

Both shook their heads, no and thanked him. "Later," said "Fabe." "After the Regimental Muster tonight." Bailey Brown grinned, took a sip, and with a wave, was off to corner the potential recruits across the road. After Brown departed, Ben said,"Wow, he seems very impatient to get the war started, 'Fabe.'"

"Ben, what you hear and see in T. Bailey Brown we see in many others these days. There has been so much spitefulness, so much angry talking and shouting."

"Nobody's around ... nobody still alive, who remembers the horrors of the Revolutionary War.

"Battle lines are being drawn up; challenges on both sides; even Bailey Brown challenged you. What do you think he would have done if you called him, 'Thorny' again tonight? He'd of probably shot you.

"Ben," "Fabe" predicted, "I have started a diary, and you will have some day a few pages to share with others in your time; some tearful observations, some vivid memories of the battlefield."

He continued, "They say time heals all mental wounds. Well, I'm not against the healing part as long as people remember wars are started by a few and engulf so many ... each life lost is a statement; each battle fought a page in a bloody chapter of our Nation's stormy history."

"Fabe" grabbed Ben's arm. His mood suddenly changed to a lighter one. "Hey, c'mon, Ben. Let's go over to the rally and see what's going on right now."

They both crossed the road together to the large grassy clearing. It was now late in the afternoon on this warm May day, sunny with temperatures in the 60's. A crowd of about 80 men and women had gathered with many waving Union flags in view.

"Captain Latham, Captain Latham," called out "Fabe" to the newly elected captain of the pro-Union Grafton Guards.

"Y'all are to stay away from them now. If you have to go to Grafton or are ordered there, you go the back way towards Webster.

"We have a report from a woman in Bridgeport that some of the "Harrison Rifles" are headin' thisaway to join other Rebels at the bridge."

At that point, T. Bailey Brown could keep still no longer. His jaws were set. Ben noticed Bailey's cheek bones stood out. Brown's tired eyes narrowed. Then Bailey interrupted Latham with: "Dammit, Cap'n; we kin take on the whole bunch o' Rebs hidin' out at the bridge, the yaller bellies. Let's do it, now!"

Latham turned on Brown and raised his voice.

"That's exactly what we don't want to do, Brown. You'll be one of the first I call when there's fightin' to be done, but not yet, not yet."

With that admonishment, Latham turned to Lt. Wilson. In low tones so Lt. Cather, Lt. Wilson, and also Ben could hear.

"Lieutenant, see that Bailey and the few others that also need it, git some instruction on discipline tommarra." The junior officers nodded.

In a louder voice to stifle the numerous murmurs going around in the church parlor, their captain continued:

“Now men, listen up! One more thing you should know ... I will be going to Wheeling, Tuesday next to sign us up, muster us into federal service.”

There was dead silence in the meeting place.

“That means we must do ourselves proud an’ stay away from startin’ any fights ‘til we get official orders from the Army. And while I’m gone with Lt. Cather for thet purpose, Lt. Wilson will be in charge.

“Any questions? Aw’ right, you’re dismissed.” Lieutenants, you and Ben stay for a few minutes,” the captain concluded.

After the others were out of earshot, Latham shook his head and said, “We have to control Bailey Brown and some of the others before they become dead heroes and no use to us.”

“Captain,” Wilson responded. “Sir, I could use a good aide.”

“Good,” said Latham with a smile as the four men left the church. “Even make him your right-hand man, even a bodyguard, Lt. Wilson.”

After a round of laughter by them, they crossed the street to inspect the first picket shift and headed towards the village green where they were joined by Sarah and her husband.

Sarah recognized Ben among them. “Well Ben, what do you think of us, now?”

Ben shook his head and replied, “It all seems so, so unreal, so confusing!”

“Come,” said “Fabe.” “It is almost midnight. Let me escort you back to Widow Poling’s. There, you will be safe overnight.” He saluted his superior officer, Latham and said, “Captain Latham, afterwards, after dropping Ben on the widow’s door step, by your leave, sir, I’ll make sure the pickets are instructed and in place.”

Latham nodded affirmatively.

Then, as “Fabe” and Ben walked away, Cather smiled and said, “Lt. Wilson, I suggest, sir, you best be checking in on your bodyguard. He may need some rescuing.”

All, including Sarah knew who “Fabe” meant, and they all laughed heartily.

And, so it was left ... as Ben retired for the night and for some days ahead, the next course of events would include Captain Latham’s trip to Wheeling next Tuesday, May 21st.

There he would be officially received by a Federal Army muster officer, a Major Oates.

Soon afterwards, on May 25, 1861 ... to be exact, the United States Army would then designate the Grafton Guards, all of Latham’s men, as B Company of the

Union's 2nd Virginia Volunteers, Infantry. Soon afterwards, Lt. Cather and his fellow soldiers would be entrained from Valley Falls and undergo training in Wheeling ... **All except one, that is,** who more than anyone else wanted to serve, but fate would have it another way.

In Latham's absence from Taylor County, the unexpected, some bad things happened, as we shall soon see.

~~~~~~~~~~~~
~~~~~~~~~~~~

CHAPTER 5

Living in Fear and Turmoil

Ben drifted off into sleep very quickly. As the townspeople protected their possessions and families from possible bushwhacker raids and thievery, Ben dreamt he was on a war front somewhere fighting alongside Bailey Brown and "Fabe" Cather.

He tossed and turned and as he saw the flash of the mouth of a gun barrel pointed at him, "argghh," he shouted and woke up. It was the next morning: May 16, still 1861.

At his side was Sarah. "You've been sleepin' a long time, Ben; you must get up," She said.

Ben looked around. He was groggy. "After you get awake, I'll explain, she added. "Come to the kitchen. Wash up and have some Pigeon Pie and fritters. You must be hungry." (Unnoticed, she slipped some Jeff Davis Pie in with the Pigeon Pie.)

At the kitchen table, Ben didn't know what to expect. Things had been moving so fast.

Sarah was there alone. Ben was hungry. As he ate, she seemed to be reading his mind. "You are still in 1861, Ben. Your travels had a way of tiring you out and stretchin' your sleep time," she said with a chuckle.

Ben took a long drink of the chicory coffee. "So, what is next?" he asked.

Sarah smiled again. "Patience, Ben, patience. I must tell you your days here are limited, so we must work fast in the short time you have in this time. George Latham left word that you can help Lt. Wilson and Private Brown in his absence. George had to go to Fairmont to get orders from Francis Pierpont."

That hot head, Bailey Brown! What's next? he thought.

Ben got up quickly and went to the door. He opened it. Where the flea market field had once been, was supposed to be and also his car, now a stable of horses and little children playing hoop stick along a one-lane dusty road.

Just at that moment, Ben began to feel very dizzy. He grabbed the door knob and hung on.The room reeled around and around, as it did just after he ate the first Pie in the old jailhouse museum.

The new piece of "Jeff Davis Pie" was now starting to take effect.

"Sarah! Sarah! My vision ... I'm losing it. I can't see you very well and the room is spinning and spinning," his voice trailed ... he fainted.

Then the motion stopped. It was very quiet except he heard a bird, a male wren trying to coax a female to the male wren's nesting site. A cool breeze was blowing. It was mid-afternoon, and there was the flea market; the crowds as he had left them in the 21st century, and he awoke in his car where it had first been parked. Ben drove home to Jan, daring not to say anything about his adventure. After all, he thought, who including Jan, would believe him?

That night, fast asleep, who should come to Ben in a dream?

It was Sarah!

Sarah spoke first in his dream ... "Ben, I'm sorry but the pie effects had worn off, and I had to give you another piece to get you back to the 21st Century. But you see, there are two other chances available for you if you want to come back."

"Oh yes, yes I do want to return. No, I don't see! Please explain," Ben mumbled ... being more confused than ever.

Sarah's image explained further: "Ben, look in the box, the box you bought from the market. In it you'll find a recipe for 'Jeff Davis Pie.' You have two more opportunities to travel back. So, do exactly as I say."

“First, pick the date and place in the past. Here are the conditions. The dates and places have to be those where first-time Civil War events happened.”

“First time,” muttered Ben aloud in his sleep, so loud in fact, Jan stirred beside him.

Sarah continued. “Yes, remember the exact date and place. Next, make the pie. Then, on the same day, go to the place where the Civil War event previously occurred, and you’ll return to us.

“It is vital you have the historic date fixed in your mind when you eat the pie and also necessary you concentrate and envision the exact place where the event occurred.”

With that reminder, she was gone; and Ben woke from his deep sleep.

It was 5 AM, but he couldn’t go back to sleep.

After tossing for an hour or more, Ben got up. He put on his slippers and went downstairs. At his history bookcase, he picked out one ... a book that described events in 1861 in western Virginia.

~~~~~~~~~~~~~~~~~~~~~~~~
~~~~~~~~~~~~~~~~~~~~~~~~

CHAPTER 6

Rendezvous in Fetterman

Ben opened the book to a chapter entitled: "Western Virginia Responds." He read:

"And while Captain George Latham was in Wheeling on May 22, the day before the big election day, Lt. Wilson and Pvt. T. Bailey Brown were headed out of Pruntytown toward Fetterman. Brown was Wilson's designated bodyguard. Ben chuckled as he remembered Bailey's outburst one night.

"It was Lt. Wilson who first saw the Confederate pickets at the covered bridge and heard the challenge by the Rebel, Daniel Knight. Wilson ordered Bailey Brown to fire and Brown did so, hitting Knight in the ear."

Ben was touched with emotion after he read the next lines ..." The shot wounded Knight and so infuriated him, he leveled his musket at Brown and emptied three slugs, hitting Brown squarely in the chest area."

Ben read further:

"Brown died almost instantly, becoming the first Civil War soldier to die from gunshot at the hands of the enemy."

Ben was touched with feeling for Bailey Brown because he felt he knew Brown, personally. It seemed to Ben he had just shook hands with Brown at the Pruntytown Union rally!

Ben put the book down."There is where I want to go. Back to May 22 and that year to see for myself what really happened."

He picked up the cigar box, opened it, looked for the recipe for "Jeff Davis Pie." After he found it, he read carefully the directions.

Ben went to the kitchen and got the ingredients together. It took him a while to find cinnamon, walnuts, and nutmeg at that hour of the morning, but he did. He prepared the pie dough and divided it in three small pans.

He whipped up the raw mixture and cooked it over low heat as the recipe called for and finished the preparation by transferring the heated contents to the three pie shells.

Then he looked up and was startled to see his wife, Jan standing in the doorway in her robe.

With arms folded, still half asleep, she looked warily at him, and said: "What? What in the world are you up to, Ben?"

Ben smiled sheepishly. "Oh Jan! You caught me ... cookin' up a little surprise ... ah, I wanted to cook breakfast for you," he fibbed.

"Here, now that you came down early and spoiled my surprise, try some," he added as he offered her a cooled dish containing the pie.

Ben knew very well that, according to Sarah, nothing strange would happen here and now since they hadn't given thought to a prior date or event where something historically happened in their present location.

Jan took a seat at the table. Pie for breakfast? She was still leery of what Ben was up to but said no more about it. Unexplainable male behavior, she concluded ... Like last Monday, when for no clear reason he brought me two pink carnations!

Ben served her a dish of the pie and a glass of milk. He then took a seat across from her as she slowly took a mouthful.

"Why, this is delicious, Ben," Jan said. "Thank you."

Ben nodded affirmatively as he slowly sampled a forkful, not knowing, himself, what to expect.

“Where did you get that recipe, Ben?”

“Oh, at the flea market yesterday,” Ben answered his wife. He beamed across the table at her, flushed with the feeling of his culinary success. “Its called ‘Jeff Davis Pie.’ ”

Jan remarked, “Good southern name ... good southern dish.Why the name?”

“No, a northern, Yankee dish,” Ben replied. “And I didn’t get a chance to ask them why. ”

“Them?” she repeated. “Yankee?” she asked.

“Huh—ah, yeah— them Yankee Cathers who fought in the Civil War,” he blurted out automatically and wished he hadn’t.”

Jan shook her head. Something he read somewhere, she thought. Misnamed pie; Civil War Cathers ... She got up and laughed, not buying his story. “Ben, You get cleaned up and dressed; and tend to your early morning household chores, Dear, and I’ll make us some coffee and pancakes.”

Ben thought that was a real winner, a means to escape, and get him off the hook from further embarrassment. He quickly went upstairs to shower, shave, and dress to avoid any more questions. But, he wondered: she’s got a good point; why do they call the mysterious pie that?

Then he went about his chores: to take out the trash and straighten up the patio and side porch.

Jan went about making the breakfast in the kitchen. About an hour later, "Its ready," she called. It was about 7:30.

After they finished it was about 8:45. Ben cleared away the dishes."Great breakfast, Jan," he said. He went to the downstairs bathroom where he brushed his teeth.

Then Ben told Jan he needed to go to Grafton and asked, "Do, you need anything from a store? I'm going to the library there." He did have a book to return, so he wasn't fibbing about that.

"Oh, no Dear; nothing from the stores. Find out some more about that mysterious Rebel pie the Yankees liked so much," Jan teased.

Ben laughed and kissed his wife on the lips and headed for Grafton. Unknown to Jan, he had slipped the remaining covered, pie plate of "Jeff Davis Pie" in a plastic bag and called over his shoulder, "Be back in about two or three hours."

He still didn't dare tell anyone about Sarah and the secret powers of "Jeff Davis Pie". And now he began to wonder:

"Damn! Why do they call it that ...?" he asked out loud.

Off he went, driving past Pruntytown and yesterday's flea market. He thought of Widow Poling's house and of the meetings with "Fabe," Captain Latham, and the others. Ben hoped Sarah was right about going back to be with Latham's Grafton Guards.

He continued on US Route 50 until he came to the bridge across the Tygarts River. He stopped at a wayside marker. It was one dedicated to the fall of Bailey Brown!

"Well this is the place," Ben whispered, even though there was no one around to hear him. He got out of his parked car and read from the marker:

"Dedicated to the memory of Thornsbury Bailey Brown ... First Union soldier killed in the Civil War.

"He lost his life on this spot May 22, 1861."

Ben concentrated on the date. He could see the numbers pictured in his mind. He projected on the supposed scene at that time ... a dark night; the covered bridge over the Tygart Valley River, now long since gone. He quickly ate most of the pie and waited and he waited.

The wait gave Ben an opportunity to think about Brown. Ben shuddered and held back a tear. T. Bailey Brown had been a special acquaintance. Just this morning, Ben had read some things about Bailey Brown's personal life.

And Sarah had given Ben a profile of Bailey and the Brown family. She and her son, "Fabe" knew Bailey Brown's widow, Nancy, quite well. Bailey, his wife and their five children had moved to the Flemington vicinity, near the Cathers in May of 1860. The Browns had come from Preston County, near Independence, where Bailey Brown was born on May 15, 1829.

Up to the beginning of hostilities in 1861, Brown worked for local farmers in the Flemington area. He also did odd jobs and had a small homestead farm and woods of his own. His modest place was in nearby Fairview (Aston) in Taylor County, where he hunted, farmed and raised a few livestock.

The exuberant Brown, proudly independent, could effectively recruit in the area for Captain Latham and the Union. Young men of the Pruntytown area readily took to Brown's rough, homespun ways. As a recruiter, he spoke plainly, with frank honesty from the heart.

Brown's confidence, his passion for the Union cause were accepted by the crowds at the Grafton and Pruntytown musters and infected the undecided with a Yankee high.

Brown's shiny new pistol and well-tailored uniform set a winning military example in the days when many volunteer soldier boys still carried Revolutionary War muskets and came to war dressed in civilian clothes ... many of them not ever before seeing or wearing underwear until they joined the Service.

"Strange" said Ben out loud. "Bailey wasn't afraid to brandish his new shooter in a crowd. I certainly wouldn't want to have faced him on the battlefield."

Then he thought about the others at the musters he saw. A few in the Flemington area he had noticed had been for the South. A few in Taylor County had slaves. But most in the county were against slavery. And wasn't there a Union safe house later in the war located in Pruntytown?

Ben's mind wandered back to thinking about Brown. He could be impulsive at times. Ben remembered their frosty introduction and how afterwards he recklessly fired his pistol in the air. He definitely exhibited an itchy trigger finger.

Unruly at times, but obedient to the end. In fact, one might say, he was obedient to a fault. "Obedience to orders may have cost him his life, prematurely," Ben sighed.

But enough day-dreaming about T. Bailey Brown, Ben thought. Nothing has happened to me. Fifteen minutes had gone by; still nothing. Thirty, then sixty minutes passed and no dizziness; none of the other "Jeff Davis Pie" symptoms he had at Prunytown!

"Nuts!" the disappointed Ben said aloud. "Its not working. Its not working!"

"What an absolute fool I am," he said to himself. "To waste my time on last night's dream."

He was about ready to jump in his car and leave. Then another vehicle stopped. It was a late model pickup truck.

“Hey Ben!” the driver called to him. It was Sarah again!

What was she doing here? What did she want now with me? Ben wondered. “W’-w-well, I guess the jokes on me,” he stammered back, too embarrassed to be very angry.

“Ben, remember what I said about being at the right place! This is **not** the spot where Brown was killed. Some years ago the County officials moved the marker and put it here. They did not put another marker at the spot where he fell that night. Let me show you where that was.”

Sarah then unrolled a small map showing the place across the river near the tracks where T. Bailey Brown fell and was immortalized.

“Come, I’ll take you where that exact spot is. Remember, you have used up two of your three chances to go back. Are you sure you want to repeat your wish or do you want to return, perhaps, to another place ... a more safe place in another time?”

She grabbed his arm. “Ben, do you have any pie left?”

At this point, Ben was unsure. “ Yes, I have some left. But I don’t know ... What if I can’t get back?”

Sarah replied. "Well, I have to tell you. You may be on an active battlefield. There is that risk of not getting back. You must be at the starting point when the pie effects wear off. Remember your portal of entry, where I'm taking you, and remember to save a final piece for the journey back to your world."

"And then of course, you might get shot on the battle-field."

Ben trembled. "A cheery thought, Sarah. A little adventure is one thing; danger and death quite another."

Did he begin to have second thoughts about leaving his peaceful surroundings for one of war? (Wouldn't you?) "Show me this historic place where he fell, Sarah. I'll let you know. I have to think about it."

Sarah beckoned to him. "Ben, follow me across Route 50 in your car." She then led Ben over the highway bridge eastward, across the river at Fetterman and turned right, onto Railroad Street. They parked across the tracks on the edge of the old narrow road.

He was now on the east side of the river. There were houses that dated back to the last century. He got out of his car and noticed the grassy approach to the west; no covered bridge, only pilings in the river of a bridge that once was and the sloping river bank, beyond.

Sarah pointed to the remnants of the old covered bridge, the stone abutments that once carried the roofed span. These piers in the water now daily go unnoticed in the shadow of the new 21st century bridge they just crossed.

“Stone and mortar always stand the tests of time,” she sighed. “Here, Ben is where T. Bailey Brown was shot ...In the middle of this road, just below the track leading into Grafton. He fell just across the road about a hundred yards from the covered bridge, your portal of entry here at Fetterman.” Sarah walked to the exact spot as she spoke. There was no marker for the public.

“Well, at the very least the County Commission could have a reference marker on Route 50 and a locator marker here,“ Ben said.

“Ben, they don’t care; they don’t care; they don’t think anyone else, especially their voting public cares,” she responded.

Sarah asked, “Well what about it ... Do you want to go back or not?”

He nodded his head and said: “Yes, I’ve gone this far. I feel the need.”

“Ben, good. Now, you know why you were chosen in the first place at Pruntytown. I have to leave you now,” she added. “My son, ‘Fabe’ Cather will be waiting for you. Remember, he is the only one who understands where you come from and how you transition, and as long as the pie effects last, this time you’ll be invisible to everyone else on the other side.”

~~~~~~~~~~~~~
~~~~~~~~~~~~~

Fig 1 — Thornsbury Bailey Brown; the photo was probably taken at the time of his birthday, May 15,1861 ... about a week before his death.

CHAPTER 7

A Salute to T. Bailey Brown

All at once Ben became dizzy and weak. The street was swirling around him. He was thrown across the road and landed on the grassy approach to the old bridge crossing. There before his eyes, a blurred timbered structure loomed before him to the West. Then, as his vision cleared, the old Fetterman covered bridge took shape before his eyes!

It was almost dark. Ben motioned to the old man at the bridge opening, about 25 feet away, "Sir, could you tell me what time it is?"

The toll booth operator, Michael Donohue, seemed to ignore him. Ben repeated his question. Still no answer; no reaction from the toll taker. Must be blind and deaf, Ben thought. Oh, that's right, he can't see me.

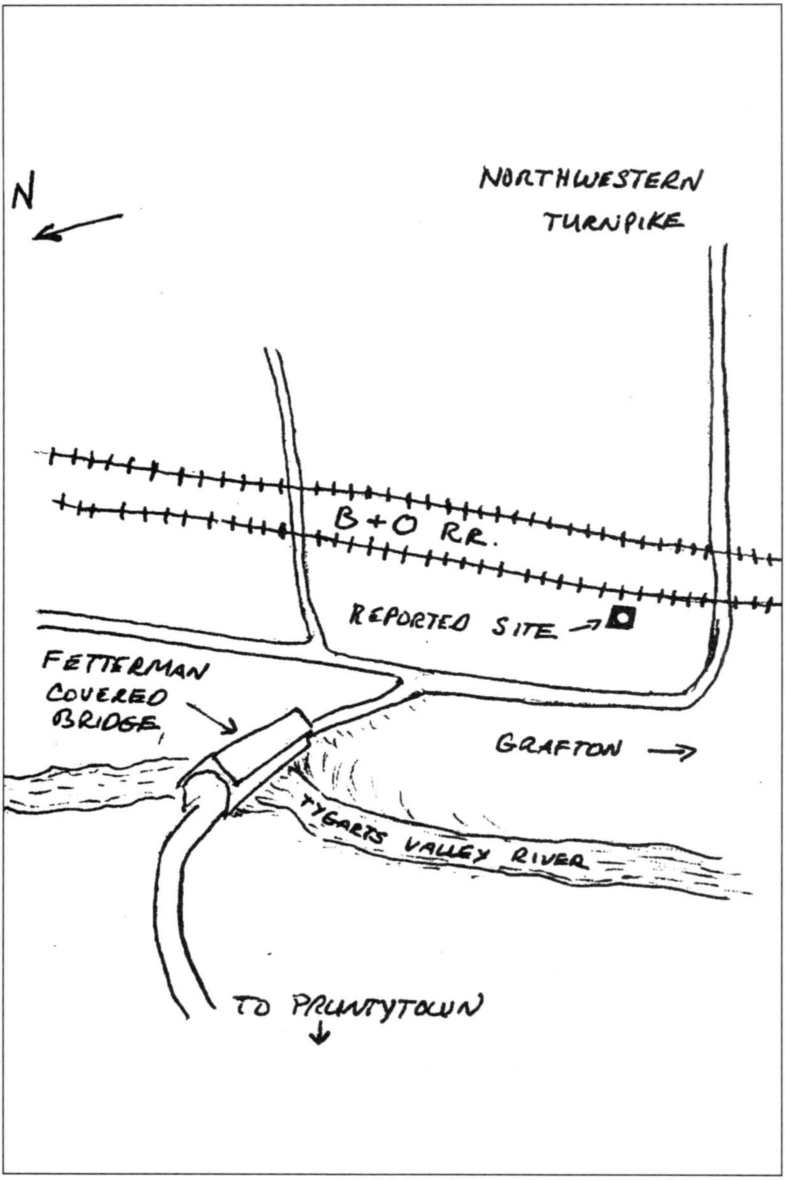

Fig 2—Location near the former Fetterman covered bridge in Taylor County where T. Bailey Brown was fatally wounded by a Confederate picket.

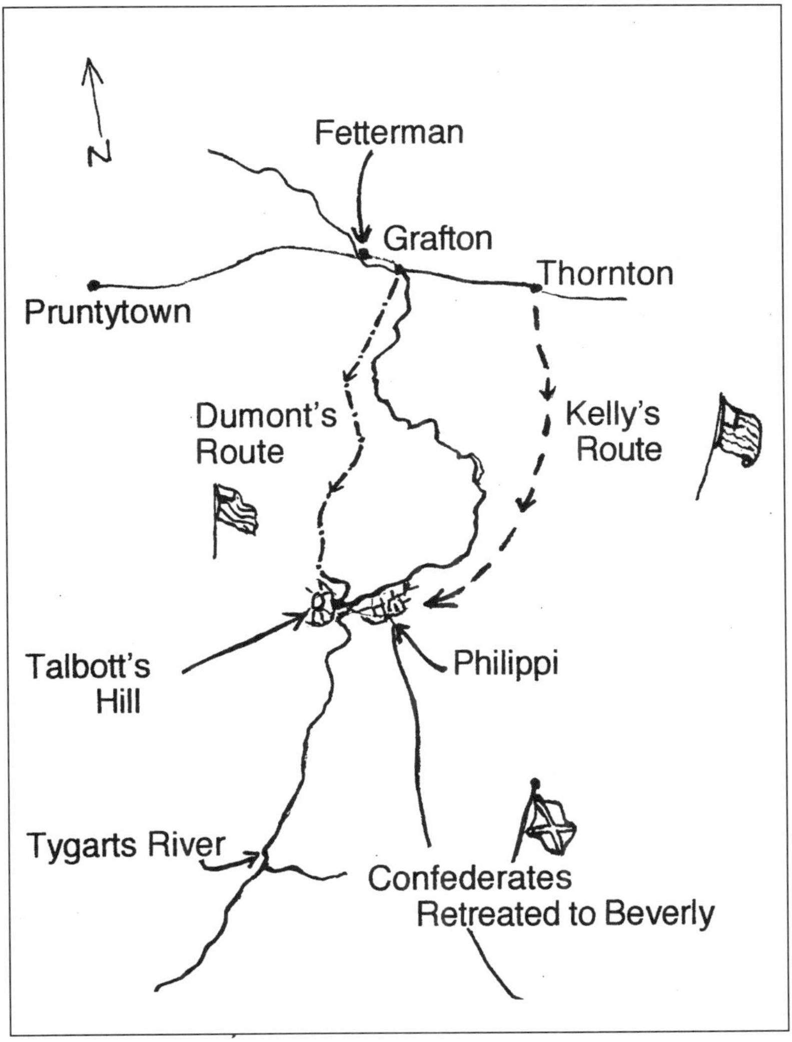

Fig 3—Prelude to"The Philippi Races" on June 3, 1861.Dumont's brigade of 1,500 rode by rail to Webster and "quick marched" the remaining 7 miles to the Philippi covered bridge. Kelly with his 1,500 men, came from Thornton and entered Philippi from the east.

Then through the darken bridge opening came a rider on horseback. The young man in a Yankee uniform handed the toll man a slip of paper without getting off his horse and said, “Thanks, Michael.”

I know that voice, thought Ben. It was “Fabe” Cather’s!

“Fabe” rode to where Ben was standing. In a low voice he said, “Ben, hello again. I can explain the bridge tender. He can not see you; no one else can either on this visit of yours from the other side. It’s safer for you. Mother asked; willed it for your protection.

“So, when we talk it has to be away from others. Otherwise, they will think I’m talking to myself.”

Ben smiled. He understood. Ben was what people of that time, from any time for that matter, would call ... “a spirit, a ghost!”

Cather waved to the watching bridge tender. “Just letting my horse have some grass,” he said; and continued out of earshot of Mr. Donohue, the toll taker. “Ben, it is all quiet around here now. But you should have seen it a couple of days ago, on May 22 and 23.”

“So, it is May again in 1861?” Ben asked.

“Here, let me help you up on Max,” “Fabe” answered. “C’mon, we’ll ride a ways, and I’ll fill you in on what has happened.”

It was exactly 18 days since Ben had been at the Pruntytown rallies and musters. Now, it was the early evening of June 2nd; 1861.

"Oh, so much to tell and so little time before we must ride," "Fabe" said as he stopped his horse at a small empty cottage about 300 yards south of the bridge. "Here, let's stop. It's empty and dry inside." The house was Pvt. Jackson Cooper's, a Grafton Guard, who had left for duty in Webster.

Once inside, Ben remembered something that was bugging him. "Oh 'Fabe', I have to ask you ... The powers of the pie; what are they?"

"Fabe's" spirit studied his friend's face for a moment. "Ben, after eating it, the pie effects people in various ways, from a gentle dream to a trip in time. It all depends on the pie-maker. The will of the person who makes the pie can be compulsively conveyed to another."

But Ben couldn't understand this, so he rattled on. "And, 'Fabe' why the name, 'Jeff Davis Pie'? Why do you Yankees give your good food Confederate names?"

Cather laughed. "Only this spell-binding food, Ben ... Only this one, Ben. Oh, Its good, all right ... good for foolin Rebs. It goes back to Davis' days at West Point when brandy got him in trouble, and he blamed it on Benny Haven's pie.Too many questions." He evaded Ben further. "You'll find those answers in your box you bought from my mother at the flea market."

Ben answered facetiously, “Yeah, right ... If I ever get back alive to read them.”

“Well, Ben you still have time to go back. Just wait by the bridge til the pie effects wear off ...”

“No. No!” Ben responded. And he changed the subject. “Poor Bailey Brown.”

“Yes,” Lt. Cather responded. “A real hero ... He didn’t know what hit him. He was with Lt. Daniel Wilson, you know.”

“I’ve read many versions of how it happened ... his death, ‘Fabe.’ But, what really did happen?”

Lt. Cather responded. “He and Wilson had just returned from Pruntytown. It was a rainy night like this one ... about 9 o’clock. It was later than they expected so they decided to take the shorter route to Grafton rather than walk the eastern road to town. No horses ... It is a mystery to me why they were walking in the first place, and apparently Wilson had no gun! At least that is what was in the report I saw.

“Anyway, there they were; anxious to return to Grafton to be with the Grafton Guard detail to prevent Letcher’s guards from frightening the voters and the women and children the next day, which was general election day, May 23.

“You remember Captain Latham went to Wheeling to get us mustered in as a regular US Army Company, and he left Wilson, the next in command, in charge.”

"There was fear for the voters all over. Why, I even heard tell that Francis Pierpont was spirited out of Fairmont the night before and didn't get to vote, himself.

"And here in Fetterman and Grafton, Robinson and his Confederate company it was feared, would come and terrorize the people and disrupt the voting here."

Cather continued. "We can't be sure of all the details, but according to Wilson, as they walked the track across the railroad bridge, the two of them were spotted by Rebel pickets. One of the pickets, Pvt. W.S. Knight called out: 'Stop, Stop, Don't go there.' Brown replied he was a private citizen and had walked this track many times before and was not going to turn back now.

"You see, Brown had come this way weeks ago, before the Rebels had taken over this bridge. Now they even had another company from Clarksburg as reinforcements, unknown to the boys on our side that night.

"Brown was defiant. On principle, he was right! The track belonged to the B&O Railroad Company and not a bunch of strangers from the outskirts of Taylor County. And on principle, he met his death, Ben! He became a symbol of what we stood for. His death really brought out the voters the next day.

"Bailey took out his shiny new pistol and on Lt. Wilson's order, fired. He missed, hitting Knight's ear but Knight didn't; with a rusty, old smooth bore relic from a Preston

County farm. Wilson was dazed and couldn't believe it at first. Then he realized his own danger and ran for town; a shot from another Rebel picket, Pvt. George Glenn, hit Wilson in the heel of his shoe.

"Long after the war Wilson would laugh at the shot off heel incident but not at the killing of T.Bailey Brown. Lt. Wilson often said had he not ordered Bailey to open fire at Knight, Brown would not have been shot and killed that night.

"The news of Brown's death quickly spread all over. The next day his body was brought back to Grafton, and a service was held for him. His death was a rallying point for all voters on the 23rd, that next day.

"So even in death, Thornsbury Bailey Brown was mustering support for independence of western counties from the Commonwealth of Virginia. His sad death, his martyrdom, became a Northern symbol to stand for our flag, our country, and strengthened our determination to fight for the Union. I'm told," Lt. Cather finished, "that on the day of voting and mourning for Brown, only one person in Grafton voted to stay with Virginia and Jeff Davis' Confederacy."

Ben sighed, "Little did Bailey Brown realize that on that night after he left Pruntytown with Lt. Wilson he would never see his family again."

"Right," "Fabe" agreed. "In fact, his youngest son, also named Bailey, was never to see his father, alive."

"That son would be born posthumously, six months, from now in November, 1861. He, with other relatives will be present at this very spot in May, 1928 for the dedication of his father's monument."

Ben marveled, "Here we are in June, 1861. How do you keep straight all the things about to happen and those in your future that did?"

"Fabe" laughed. "Your question sounds like something from 'Alice in Wonderland.' It's too much for you computer literate mortals to understand. One way perhaps to grasp it, is to accept the fact we operate with different soft ware on the other side, and any time can be the past, present, or the future for us.

"But this chatter is not getting us to Philippi. So let's mount up and be on our way, Ben."

They left the cottage and traveled by horseback to Webster, which would later this month be the main Union Command Post of Major General George McClellan. His headquarters would be housed in the future Anna Jarvis home.

Back in 1861 under Col. Porterfield, the Rebels had blown up several small bridges on or about May 26 in Mannington and Farmington and made a mild threat to cut transportation and communications between the White House and the Union forces to the West.

Ben did not know it, but Colonel B. F. Kelly with Union reinforcements, was ordered on May 27th to travel by rail from Wheeling to Grafton with his regiment. That same day saw Confederates under Captain Christian Roberts destroying bridges and culverts to the east.

Roberts was killed in a skirmish with an Ohio unit, and he thus, became the first Confederate soldier and officer killed by enemy fire anywhere in the war.

Kelly was aware of imminent plans of the Confederate, Porterfield to attack Latham's company in Grafton. However, the Rebel colonel received some intelligence from a woman spy revealing federal reinforcements were on their way from Wheeling.

Another Union force, a brigade of Indiana volunteers under General Morris, poised a few days before on the Ohio at Parkersburg, was also under way by rail. And now, Morris was close to Clarksburg, heading east where he would join Kelly in Grafton on June 1 to take overall command of Union forces in western Virginia.

With the news of Yankee build up at Grafton, Porterfield withdrew his forces from that city and moved them about June 1 to Philippi, about 30 miles southeast, just before Ben arrived at the Fetterman scene. There, in Philippi, the Confederates felt safe and took up temporary residences in local houses. Some infantry were quartered in the Barbour County courthouse.

Nearby, were comrades in arms; two companies of Barbour Grays and Upshur Grays, sons and husbands of the local town folk. Most of Porterfield's estimated 1,000 troops in the Philippi area were green, inexperienced volunteers, poorly equipped for war.

General Morris and his men had arrived yesterday. He was made the first, overall Commander of Union forces in western Virginia. The General had heard of Col. Kelly's plan to attack Porterfield in Philippi. Morris approved; in fact enlarged upon it, by ordering Col. Dumont of the 7th Indiana Brigade to support Kelly with a second column.

In the scheme of maneuver, Dumont's units would travel by rail to Webster and wait for nightfall. At the same time, Kelly and his men would march from Thornton in the east toward Philippi in a separate, somewhat parallel column, about 12 miles away. (Figure 3, pg 51)

Now, it was still early evening on June 2nd about 8:30 PM, and Dumont gave the order to quick march along the Beverly Pike, about five miles north of their objective. And, Ben was about to see some of this repeat of history this over night march in the rain along the Grafton-Webster Pike where he would arrive before the first shot was fired to witness a historic first in Philippi early the next day.

As "Fabe" was relating these events, a courier rode up and told "Fabe" to get ready to ride north.

~~~~~~~~~~~~~~~~
~~~~~~~~~~~~~~~~

CHAPTER 8

Six-pounders Overhead—

Suddenly, Ben found himself alone in a strange place. "Fabe" had vanished! was gone, disappeared; without any trace of his Civil War friend, or his horse. Ben trembled and felt lost. Then he remembered no one else could see him in this life in 1861. He could hear voices; he could see lanterns lit. It was raining very hard. He was no longer in Fetterman.

Ben looked at his watch; it was about 4 AM.

He moved forward toward the light. Around a smoky lantern under a makeshift 4-walled canopy were three soldiers. It was outside a tent. An outpost, Ben thought; an orderly room in the field maybe, he surmised. The three soldiers were sitting on dry logs under the canopy which was pitched on the grounds in front of the Barbour County courthouse. They were confederates.

The building fronted Main Street in Philippi. Many of the other Rebels were asleep inside the courthouse and also in the covered bridge.

"Con ... Confederates!" he muttered softly out loud with surprise.

"Yuh hear that? Like someone talking," asked one. His name was George Glenn.

"Nah, only wind an' rain; just your nerves," said another, whose name was Bill Reese. "Remember we have lookouts and neighbor folk around. There's no Yanks out there to worry about on this wretched night."

"He's right, George," said Daniel, the third Rebel, who was working on his cartridge belt. The three had just gotten here a day earlier from Fetterman in Taylor County.

A fourth Rebel then joined them with invisible Ben able to hear every word. He was Perry Keener and a new, very wet recruit in this Co A of the the 25th Virginia Infantry Regiment.

Keener was on duty tonight as a picket at the covered bridge on the west bank. The others were also detailed to the watch. "Whew," he said. "It's really hard to see out there. I'm soaking wet. No Yanks will come around tonight. So, I think I'll stay here and dry off."

Unknown to them, Porterfield had called off the picket details himself, because of the weather.

Daniel looked up from his cartridge belt. “New man, hey? Well, I’d say you’ve done enough for one day. Here, get yourself dried off and have some coffee and a piece of this pie. One nice thing about Philippi is all the ‘seceshes’ (secessionists) around ...

“See all those tents by the bridge?” He continued. “Barbour and Upshur Grays in all ‘em. Locals, too ... which means their wives and girl friends are willing to cook and wait on us.”

The new recruit needed no second invitation to pull up a log and prop his bed roll on it for a seat at the cozy fire. After getting situated, he poured a cup of coffee and tasted the pie. He exclaimed, “Hmmm, that’s quite good. What’s it called?”

Daniel smiled and replied. “Oh, some good, old, cooked rabbit in a pan of gravy. The lady who brought it over said it was ‘Belgium Hare.’ We all thought it was good, too.”

Pvt. Keener glanced at Daniel’s bandaged head. “Say, what happened to you? Did some jealous husband catch up with yuh?”

Pvt. George Glenn broke out with a muffled laugh ... “He got an earful; a real earful .... in the line of duty, I might add ... over at Fetter ...” But George never finished his sentence.

Because, all at once a pistol shot was heard. It came from across the river in the west.

“The signal ... Its the signal!” yelled Bill. “We’re being attacked! ... must get all the men up.”

The four scrambled to arouse the other sleeping Confederates. Ben knew the Union forces were close by.

And, the first land battle of the Civil War was on.

The Union plan had called for Dumont to position his troops, in those early morning hours of June 3, on the western shore and occupy the covered bridge.

The main attack was to come east of town, from Col. Kelly’s units moving from Thornton to the eastern outskirts of Philippi. This maneuver would cut off Rebels retreating to the south.

Dumont and Kelly were supported by Ohio artillery in command of Col. Landers. The battery moved to positions above the town on Talbott Hill. The cannon pieces were 6-pounders, positioned on a northwest overhead bluff.

This hill would later be a part of the campus of Alderson-Broaddus College. It is a local highly regarded college now perched above the town and bridge.

The signal for the main attack by the Federals was to come from Kelly’s force when in position east of town ...

But a strange sequence of events would unfold to change the course of events that day.

Unknown to Dumont, Kelly and his 1,500 men got lost and were delayed in the confusing rainy darkness.

When Dumont's advance Union soldiers came up Talbott's Hill, near Thomas Humphrey's farmhouse, Mrs. Humphreys saw them. Her son, Nelson, was a new member of the Barbour Grays and was in camp below. She put her other son, a 12 year old, on a horse to ride and warn her older Confederate son and Porterfield.

When Dumont's troops pulled the boy from the horse at least twice, she ran in the house and got a pistol. The courageous woman came out firing but in the dark missed the Yankee soldiers. These were the shots Ben had just heard that aroused and scattered the Confederates.

With Dumont thinking the signal was from Kelly, Dumont ordered Landers to begin firing.

With the 6-pounders whizzing over Ben's head as well as the heads of the Confederates, it didn't take the Rebels long to begin a hasty retreat, "without orders"... as the record shows.

Dumont's Union forces occupied the bridge. The only way out of town for the Rebs was to the south, toward Belington. And with little delay, the brave, but overwhelmed, surprised Confederates departed and wound up in Beverly, south of Elkins.

Col Kelly's troops did manage to arrive about ten minutes late, not soon enough to trap the Rebels in the soggy streets that night.

Kelly, though, was very angry he had been delayed and personally led his "Blue Jacket" soldiers in hot pursuit.

So close was he to gunfire, he was wounded in the chest by the Rebel noncom, Sims. It was reported later falsely, even in the newspapers, Kelly was killed. But he lived on to finish out the entire war.

Sims was captured and about to be executed by a vengeful crowd of Yanks when Kelly interceded on his stretcher and spared his shooter, saying Sims' act was in an act of war, and he was only following orders.

Ben watched the action from his safe, invisible vantage point. "Wow!" he said. "So swift was the retreat of Daniel Knight and his comrades. No wonder the first land battle of the war became known as 'The Philippi Races'."

On the Confederate side of the casualty ledger, ten or less were wounded; two of them from Company C and two from Company D.

Another of the wounded was 18 year old Pvt. James E. Hanger of the Churchville Cavalry. He was hit in one leg by a ricocheted cannon shot from a 6-pounder.

When Ben came up on the scene he noticed a Union surgeon, James Robison, of the 16th Ohio tending to Hanger. His shattered leg was amputated seven inches below the hip. Ben reached out to comfort the pain-wracked soldier. **This operation was the first battlefield amputation in the Civil War.** The first of tens of thousands, shuddered Ben, to be done over the next four years.

Overall, the fighting lasted about thirty minutes. Ben noticed the Confederates had beaten the Yankees by ten minutes in their escape from the steaming, angry Kelly and his troops.

Ben would learn later that both Kelly and Hanger would survive the war. During his convalescence, Hanger would make an artificial limb for himself from barrel staves. So successful was it, other amputees wanted them, also.

The Confederates would then commission Hanger to make more ... many more. He moved to Richmond, then later to Washington, DC.

And, as Pvt. Hanger was the first amputee, Kelly was the first Civil War field grade officer (Major or above) to be wounded in battle.

After the popular commander recovered from his wounds, Kelly was presented with a new horse by grateful followers; the mount, he named "Philippi."

The town of Philippi was wide awake early on that rain-drenched morning of June 3, 1861. It was now about 9 AM, and Ben was beginning to feel the tingling in his fingers and toes.

It was the same feeling he experienced in Pruntytown when the first "Jeff Davis Pie" effects were wearing off.

Quickly, he ran for the river. There, once again, he saw "Fabe" on horseback. Ben hailed his friend who rode up smiling. "Where were you? What happened?" Ben asked.

"Fabe" put his fingers to his hat brim as if to give Ben a jaunty salute. "Had business up North in Wheeling with my unit, Ben. My spirit was called back there. Come, jump on back." He motioned to Ben. "We must get you back to the starting point."

Then Ben remembered Sarah's reminder. When the effect wore off, he had to be at the portal of entry ... in this case, in the street, 100 yards from the covered bridge in Fetterman.

"I have a pass," "Fabe" said as they enter the Philippi covered bridge "...to get through the Union lines," he added. "Remember, Ben, they can't see you, yet."

They rode hard along the pike. It was at least thirty miles back to the Fetterman location.

Each of the five times they were stopped along the way, once at Webster "Fabe" showed his pass at each picket check point.There was no problem. Ben was still invisible. "Fabe" was highly regarded by General Morris and his staff.

Lt. Fabricius Cather had an exclusive headquarters pass.He was a top military advisor to Morris and later would become a wanted man by the Confederates. They would place a large bounty price on his head.

But now, he and Ben were fighting against time. The pie was wearing off. A half mile from Fetterman, Ben was becoming visible to anyone in sight. Just then, three Union horsemen rode up, approaching warily from the north. Ben and "Fabe" were between Grafton and Fetterman and close to the covered bridge.

"Stop, give the password, you two. Hands above your heads," one ordered. "You're all right," said the second picket, looking at "Fabe's" pass. "Wait a minute. Who's this other one with you? Why are two of you on one horse?"

"He's my aide," shot back "Fabe." "Don't, don't get too close. See how bent up he is? He's got the flux ... all loose inside and bloody, too ... with fever that spreads and kills," "Fabe" lied. They got down and backed away, their hands over their mouths.They knew about small pox.

But then one ordered, "Let's see his sick card!"

"Fabe" seized the moment and spurred his horse. "We have to go, the man's dying." They began to ride away. They got about seventy-five yards away, when the startled pickets recovered. "Wait a minute, Wait," called the third picket. "He must be listed. Everyone does!" he yelled. And, the three took off after Ben and "Fabe" to stop them.

"Fabe" pulled his horse to the left. Now, they were about 200 yards yards from the bridge, near the river bank. "Hurry, Ben," he urged. "Get down. Jump into the water and hide under the overhead willow branches, there until they're gone."

Ben got down and half-ran, half-fell down the steep bank to the water's edge.

In over his waist, he turned just in time to see "Fabe" and his horse vaporize in a puff of red smoke. Unknown to Ben, "Fabe" was again spirited back to Wheeling where members of his unit would never know he had momentarily left it.

The red smoke drifted into the faces of the three pickets who began to cough and gag and choke. The smoke had prevented them from seeing Ben scramble to the bank and slide down to the water. It gave him the opportunity to hide.

Ben stooped quietly in the water, with all except for his face beneath, under the overhanging, protective willow branches.

One of the pickets muttered, "They must be here somewhere, maybe hiding in the brush, yonder." He pointed up the track away from Ben's hiding place.

The three soldiers were still coughing and clearing their throats. "Hmmmph!" cried one. "That really burns m'throat, whatever it tis. Say, yuh don't think ... you don't think its the flux, do yuh?"

"Well," said the third. "Let's don't take any chances. Report 'em dead, I say, an' let's git back to the cards an' wimmen at camp."

The three pickets laughed and headed away from that spot, not fifteen feet from a wet, shivering Ben. Williams below in the water ...

He felt dejected. Here he was marooned in a different century and with no spiritual power to transition back to his time. How would he ever get past the picket at the bridge entrance?

Since he wasn't at the portal on the street when the pie effects wore off, the pie magic wouldn't take him home as was done in Pruntytown on his first time trip. He needed some more pie.

Then, he remembered something ... There was still a piece of the pie in his wet shirt pocket. It had been protected, because it was wrapped in a plastic baggie. But it must be all mashed up, he thought. He slowly, quietly waded out of the water, soaken-wet. He crawled out and lay on the bank, head down, for a moment to rest.

Next to his face, on the ground, he spied a Confederate minie ball. No doubt, dropped accidentally by one of the pickets, Ben thought. He picked it up and absent-mindedly put it in his left hand, as he carefully reached into his upper shirt pocket with his right.

It was still there, he thought. The pie! Trembling, with anticipation and shock, he felt the soggy baggie. What if there was no pie left? What if it had all washed away when his shoulders were under water? He turned on his side.

Still lying on his side, Ben pulled the baggie out of his pocket slowly. He could feel the mystical substance. He could see about one mouthful left, moist and pasty, but there, nevertheless!

He put the minie ball down and carefully with two hands teased the morsel from the wet bag. Will this work? Or am I doomed to live and die in the 19th century, he wondered.

As he raised the opened bag to his lips; he hesitated for a second, stared at the opening and then, quickly with a prayer, bolted it down, along with some entrapped river water. The flavor was familiar. It was his "Jeff Davis Pie."

At that moment, he heard a gun hammer sharply click. Ben looked up, right in the face of a Union soldier standing over him. The open end of a musket was pointed at Ben's head. How long the soldier had been there was anyone's guess.

They stared at each other for at least a minute. To Ben, it seemed like an eternity.

Then the picket spoke. “What are you doing here? Swum across, did yuh to avoid us on the bridge, huh? Get up slowly, very very slowly.” The cautious picket backed away a few feet, still aiming the musket at the wet, still dripping Ben.

Ben staggered to his feet with hands high. “Please believe me. I’m a friend: I was a friend of Bailey Brown.” “Oh yah?” the soldier exclaimed. “Well, If’n yor such a good friend ...” he hesitated, “I mean past, good friend ... what did his good friends call him?”

The picket poked Ben smartly in the ribs with his musket barrel and waited for an answer. His finger tightened on the trigger, ready to pull it in any second, in memory of his recently killed buddy. That’s right. The picket had been a good friend of T. Bailey Brown.

Ben was not getting dizzy. He was still too far from the street, the spot where Brown was killed. “Please I need some help. Please get me to the street over there. His name was ‘Thorny’.”

The picket relaxed and smiled. He raised the barrel of the musket in a less menacing direction and motioned to Ben to walk ahead of him toward the street away from the river, east of the bridge.

As he walked toward the place where Brown had died, Ben began to feel the dizziness come on. It was working, the "Jeff Davis Pie."

He could hardly see the road or tracks. He turned to look at the covered bridge.The bridge timbers began to shake and swirl around and around. Ben could hear garbled voices mixed up words with no meanings; some echoing shouts from little children at play and light, lilting laughter from grown-ups at a party or dance, where old time music was playing.

Then, there was suddenly nothing ... nothing but quiet. All was still, and then with a roar, the covered bridge vaporized and drifted away. It lifted up it front of Ben as some rolling cloud to dissipate as valley fog as Ben was hurled forward with air rushing against his face to another time ahead, to the 21st century.

Then, the motion stopped, and once again, he could hear the silence, the quiet of his surroundings. He awoke in his parked car. Alone; no one else was nearby.

He was back where he began this second trip, on the brick-lined street near the railroad tracks as it was before his Civil War experiences. He looked out over the river bank. No covered bridge; only the piers sticking out of the water. Even his clothes were dry. He shook his head to clear it. Ben was still dazed. He started his car and slowly drove home to his wife, Jan.

Back home at Maple Lake, Ben greeted his wife and went upstairs to change clothes and take a shower. It hardly seemed possible only two hours had elapsed since he had left the house. Ben checked several clocks to be sure. It was about noon.

After lunch, he sought the box, his original purchase from Sarah. He leafed through the folio and saw some pages from Lt. Cather's diary. (Author's note: The following are actual quotes from Cather's diary.) Ben sat down and then read:

"Thursday, July 12, 1861:
Our spies report General Garnet has taken command from Col. Porterfield after Porterfield's disastrous rout at Philippi, June 3 ...

"General Morris and his staff are in hot pursuit, crossing the Cheat Mountain in a heavy rain storm ... General Morris' advance column was headed by Captain Banks who overtook the enemy at Carrick's Ford. (sit Corrick's)

"Saturday, July 14, 1861:
In the battle that ensued, General Garnet was killed, the first high ranking officer in the Confederacy so far, along with 25 of his command.

"General Morris, a classmate of Garnet's at West Point, ordered his men to prepare Garnet's remains for burial."

"He dressed the body in one of his own uniforms and had it taken to Grafton where it was kept iced awaiting instructions from Richmond for its disposal.

"General Morris also ordered me to see to the decent burial of a teen-age lad who died in service as General Garnet's bodyguard. Ordering my detail to scoop out a shallow grave, we wrapped the lad in his battle flag ....

"Before lowering it to its last resting place. I said to the detail; 'Gentlemen I am a Baptist and believe in Christian burial. Allow me to offer up a prayer for the soul of this young lad who died so bravely.'

"The men, uncovering, bent the knee at the grave side, and at the end of the supplication, lowered the body into the grave and covered his face from the sight of man forever."

Ben looked up, stared into space and was confused. He was having trouble picturing what he read at home and what he had dreamt about the war. Then he read another page of Cather's diary describing more of the same day, same scene ... Cather wrote:

"My detail was ordered to collect the war property of the Confederates left on the field. Among the articles found was a leather cartridge case on which was burned the inscription: **'The property of Daniel S. Knight who killed the first Yankee in Virginia May 22, 1861.'** "

Ben sighed and said out loud, "Knight ... who killed Bailey Brown at Fetterman. Knight ... what happened to him? ... Cather doesn't say ..."

Ben looked further in the folio. Folded and beneath his "Jeff Davis Pie" recipe were two long newspaper articles in faded ink.

The first one read:
"Word has reached these parts of an elaborate scheme to defraud the honor of our brave southern troops. It seems one Union woman of questionable virtue has enticed our men to treason. Her name is Abbie McQuire who comes from a high society, New York Irish home. Beware, good soldiers. She uses the trick of bringing you a spirituous pie. 'Jeff Davis Pie', she calls it. 'Well if'n it were good nuf for Mr. Davis,' the lady vows, 'tis safe and good nuf for you.' So, noble Captain John Wood, CSA whose court martial is today took the bait from her ... Wood is accused of telling military secrets while drunk in private behind his closed office door. Well, if it wasn't the pie, that put him up to treason, heavens only knows what did get her behind his door. Laugh, Yanks! We have women, too."

——— Richmond Register, July 15, 1861"

Ben laughed. Quite foxy of the Yanks. The pie story made good propaganda using Jeff Davis' early cadet days drinking and eating habits as a ploy to get secrets. That must have tickled the Union folks. No doubt, similar stories circulated in the South, that poked fun at Lincoln and made good propaganda for the Confederates ...

Ben then saw the second story. It was called: " 'Jeff Davis Pie', Another Version."

Ben read it to himself:

"Our man in Charleston, South Carolina sends this report. A Colonel E.L., CSA. who shall be nameless, was found unconscious on the floor of his apartment by his commanding officer, General Cox who caught the woman spy in the act of poisoning our leader, Col. E. L. The Colonel told of his dinner companion, a woman named Nanette from New Orleans. 'An elegant poetress,' he called her, who was having dinner with him in his private parlor.

"She had brought a pie, 'Jeff Davis Pie', she called it. Almost at once after he ate it, 'the room began to spin around and around,' he reports. He grew weak and heard the mocking laughter by the lady.

"She called it 'Jeff Davis Pie', yes. But, dear readers, it was a Union scheme to get secrets from our Colonel, and she was no lady, only a Union spy ... While on the floor, E. L. remembers thinking about his dead grandfather in the Revolutionary War and actually seeing him in a dream when his Commanding Officer, General Cox shook him back to our world.

"Strange, indeed. We have other reports. The pie's mysterious compelling powers; its devilish ingredients make a difference, affecting different people in different ways."

"'It tasted of pleasant sweetness, with an ambrosial walnut flavor, very compelling, simply delicious,' our Colonel reported. The floor was falling away from him and the room spinning around he says, after he ate the pie."

The article Ben was reading ended with:
"Dear readers, let this be a lesson to never imbibe in an unknown pie or trust a strange woman who brings you one; especially one with the trusted, honorable name of Jeff Davis."

~~~~~~~~~~~~~~~~~~~~~~~~

After reading these two articles Ben scoffed. He thought the stories were folklore. Something made up as a cover up story. Maybe some Union woman got the better of this Rebel Colonel, and the fast-talking Colonel blamed it on some pie-in-the-sky spy plot. Chances are the General walked in and surprised them both, maybe on the floor ... with the Colonel somewhat preoccupied and indisposed ...

Ben smiled and continued to rationalize his situation. Jan has been saying I've recently been talking in my sleep, calling out " 'Fabe', Sarah, and Bailey as well as other names ... " And that's without eating any pie.

When I fell asleep and woke up twice in my own car ... those dreams I had, nothing more than that. "Ben, its your over-active sub-conscious acting up," he said aloud. "Too much reading about the Civil War. And thinking about those characters in the books."
~~~~~~~~~~~~~~~~~~~~~~~~

Ben had convinced himself there was nothing mysterious about "Jeff Davis Pie." It's like my trolley ride dream. How very, very real it seems; where I frequently take a crowded street car trolley ride, not knowing where and when to get off. I keep ridin' and ridin' and ridin'... missing my stop until I wake up frustrated ... like I woke up in my car today.

Well, I know where to get off on this 1861 kick.

Ben breathed a sigh of relief; pure fantasy, overworked imagination. What a dummy I am! He laughed at himself.

But, what a relief to know it can be explained, and that I never left the 21st century.

He heard not the first, but Jan's second call to him. "Earth calling Ben," he said out loud. Reality check time, he thought. "Yes, Dear! What do you want?" he answered back.

"Come down here, please Ben. I have something to show you."

Ben responded by heading downstairs.

"Just a dream," he mumbled. "Just a dream, he repeated, and the words sounded more reassuring that before. Ben laughed out loud. "Just a dream ... tah dah, a dream." Jan overheard him.

"What's a dream?" she shot back with a wary look at her grinning, bubbly husband.

"Ben, when are you going to learn to empty your pockets before throwing your pants and shirts in the wash? Here, this was bumping around in the dryer!!!"

She paused and then added, "What is it? Some kind of Civil War relic?"

It was the minie ball he had found earlier in the shadows of the old covered bridge that once spanned the Tygarts at Fetterman.

~~~~~~~~~~~~~~~

The End
~~~~~~~~~~~~~~~

CHAPTER 9

Shopping List of Some Other, First-time Developments in the War

As the reader is well aware, parts of past pages throughout our story have been bolded to highlight some first-time events of the war. Also noteworthy were these significant firsts.

Weaponry:

electrically triggered bombs and mines
railroad artillery
revolving gun turrets
functional machine guns; repeating rifles
land mines; flame throwers

Medical:

widespread use of anesthetics
sanitation board inspections
army ambulance corps
hospital ship
army nurses corps

Personnel:

first woman commissioned officer
first black army officer
conscription and legal voting by soldiers
army chaplains as commissioned officers

Communications:

telegraph networks
wig wag signal codes in battle
aerial drops of propaganda leaflets

Transportation:

railroad transport of troops
aircraft carriers (for balloons)
submarines

Miscellaneous, but still important:

snorkels, telescopic sights, periscope
the bugle call, "Taps"
the Medal of Honor
armored ships
smoke screens and blackouts

Horses played a new, important role in the war. Often they were treated as comrades in arms, especially those belonging to the Generals.

Gen. Robert E Lee purchased "Traveler" during one of Lee's few excursions in western Virginia near the community of Lookout. It is located west of Lewisburg, West Virginia.

Gen. B. F. Kelly was given a horse shortly after he was wounded at Philippi, Va (WVa), and to mark the occasion, he promptly named the animal, "Philippi" after that city.

Gen. J. A. J. Lightburn, one of the Union's forgotten generals, a brilliant leader and boyhood friend of "Stonewall" Jackson, was saved from certain death in the saddle early in the war when his horse, "Major" bolted as a minie ball was about to hit Lightburn in the head.

We close this section on Civil War potpourri with some unique, trademark idiosyncrasies of a few of the leaders.

Gen. "Stonewall" Jackson, the great tactician and inspirational leader, was a finicky eater. In the morning he would crave fresh raspberries.

Gen. Ambrose Burnside wore shaggy sideburns, a self-styled fashion named after him and worn widely today.

Gen. Nathan Bedford Forrest captured the attention of Gen. Robert E. Lee. When asked who was the best soldier on either side of the war, Lee was said to answer. "A man I have never seen, sir. His name is Forrest." Nathan Forrest also had a thing about horses. He was known to arrogantly brag he had killed one more Yank than the 29 horses shot from under him in battle during the war.

A Confederate postage stamp with Jeff Davis' image was almost printed until a jealous aide found out ahead of time. To prevent its printing, he confided in Mrs. Davis that it was a shame that the Davis profile had a strange likeness to "Abe" Lincoln. When the aide produced a preprint copy for her to see at a social gathering, the stamp was immediately pulled from Confederate circulation.

~~~~~~~~~~~~~~~~~~
~~~~~~~~~~~~~~~~~~

ADDITIONAL END NOTES

1) Sixty days after he was wounded, Kelly received a promotion to Brigadier General. He recovered from his chest wounds and went on to command strategic forces, including the important effective defense of the B&O railroad system for the Union. Kelly was not blamed later by his superiors for getting lost before the attack on Philippi; his delay which saved the Confederate forces that day.

2) Confederate Col. Porterfield was not so lucky. After a hearing of the matter, the Rebel rout was blamed on him, and he was soon replaced by General Garnet as Commander of Confederate forces in western Virginia.

3) After the Civil War, Hanger moved to Staunton, Virginia to continue production of artificial limbs. The company grew. In World War I, J. E. Hanger, Inc had factories in France and England. Today, the corporation is diversified and still operates world-wide.

4) The information of Brown's death and the details of events leading up it are based on fact. Details of troop movements before and during the "Philippi Races" are also factual.

5) Knight's inscribed leather cartridge case boasted of Brown's death. Some would see the coldly advertised Brown's demise as some justified trophy of war. Others might see the lost, so inscribed case as symbol of a warped sense of values and eventually, a lost cause.

6) The Confederate cartridge case was lost on an active battlefield, only to be found by Brown's good friend, Lt. Cather at Corrick's Ford on July 14, 1861... after a Yankee victory.

7) Cather, Latham, Knight, Wilson, Glenn, and Donohoe were real persons.The four Confederates at the Philippi courthouse were fictitiously placed there. However, it is well known the Rebel home guards reinforced Porterfield's troops, and Mrs. Humphreys' older son, Nelson, was one of them.

8) From all reports, Knight, Wilson, Cather, and Latham survived the war. Lt. Wilson, you will recall, was with Brown on that night, May 22, 1861. Wilson speculated afterwards, that maybe had he not given Bailey Brown the order to open fire, Brown would not have been killed that night.

9) Jan and Ben Williams were not real people.

10) Bailey Brown is seen wearing a neatly trimmed Infantry uniform in Figure 1, page 48. Quite possibly, this picture was taken on his birthday, just a week before his death.

11) Lt. Cather did not forget T. Bailey Brown. On the first anniversary of his friend's death, Cather wrote in his diary:

"Monday, May 22, 1862; This marks the anniversary of the beginning of the bloody Civil War. One year ago, today ... the ill fated Thornsbury Bailey Brown, member of the Grafton Guards, gave his life for the Union ..."

12) After the war, Anna Jarvis would later be the founder and first to promote Mother's Day as a national holiday. The building in Webster, her former home and McClellan's first headquarters in western Virginia, is preserved as a national landmark and now open to visitors, the year-around.

13) The nickname, "Thorny" was fictitious, and no disrespect was obviously intended.

14) And finally, there **is** a "Jeff Davis Pie" which does go back in folklore to the days before and during "The War Between The States"!

But, the author is not able to vouch for any special powers the pie might have on anyone who eats it!

~~~~~~~~~~~~~~~~~~~~~~~~~~~
~~~~~~~~~~~~~~~~~~~~~~~~~~~

Fig 4 — Thornsbury Bailey Brown's marker overlooks all others in the National Cemetery ... Grafton, West Virginia.

Fig 5 — The Bailey monument, misplaced on US Route 50, just west of the Tygarts Valley River and Grafton.

REFERENCES

Armstrong, George. ed 1990. "Personal Papers of G. A. Porterfield" in: *The 25th and Ninth Battalions. Richmond, VA.*

Brinkman, Charles. 1946. "American Wars and Taylor County Men." Taylor County Historical and Genealogical Society; Self-published; Grafton, WV

Brinkman, Charles. "1958 Collection." West Virginial Archives, W Va University; Morgantown, WV.

Cather, Fabricius A. 1861-65. Personal Diary, unpublished in Brinkman collection, Morgantown.

Carnes, Eva M. 1995. "Centennial History of the Philippi Covered Bridge." Barbour County Historical Society; Philippi, WV.

Cox, J. D .1887. "McClellan in West Virginia" in: *Battles and Leaders of the Civil; War,* Vol 1. Book Sales, Inc. 1989; Secaucus, NJ.

Ford, Darlene. August, 2000. Personal Communication.

Southern History Society. Vol. 16, 1888. Publication city unknown.